CALIFORNIA
HSP Math

UNIT 5

Harcourt

SCHOOL PUBLISHERS

Visit *The Learning Site!*
www.harcourtschool.com

Part Number 9997-83974-9

9 10 11 12 13 14 15   1678   16 15 14 13 12 11
4500335969

© Harcourt

Mathematics Advisor

Roger Howe
Professor of Mathematics
Yale University
New Haven, Connecticut

Senior Authors

Evan M. Maletsky
Professor Emeritus
Montclair State University
Upper Montclair, New Jersey

Joyce McLeod
Visiting Professor, Retired
Rollins College
Winter Park, Florida

Authors

Angela G. Andrews
Assistant Professor,
    Math Education
National Louis University
Lisle, Illinois

Juli K. Dixon
Associate Professor of
    Mathematics Education
University of Central Florida
Orlando, Florida

Vicki Newman
Classroom Teacher
McGaugh Elementary School
Los Alamitos Unified
    School District
Seal Beach, California

Tom Roby
Associate Professor
    of Mathematics
Director, Quantitative
    Learning Center
University of Connecticut
Storrs, Connecticut

Janet K. Scheer
Executive Director
Create-A-Vision
Foster City, California

Jennie M. Bennett
Mathematics Teacher
Houston Independent
    School District
Houston, Texas

Lynda Luckie
Director, K–12 Mathematics
Gwinnett County Public
    Schools
Suwanee, Georgia

Karen S. Norwood
Associate Professor of
    Mathematics Education
North Carolina State University
Raleigh, North Carolina

Robin C. Scarcella
Professor and Director
    Program of Academic English
    and ESL
University of California, Irvine
Irvine, California

David G. Wright
Professor
Department of Mathematics
Brigham Young University
Provo, Utah

Program Consultants and Specialists

Russell Gersten
Director, Instructional
    Research Group
Long Beach, California
Professor Emeritus of
    Special Education
University of Oregon
Eugene, Oregon

Michael DiSpezio
Writer and On-Air Host
    JASON Project
North Falmouth, Massachusetts

Tyrone Howard
Assistant Professor
UCLA Graduate School
    of Education —
    Information Studies
University of California
    at Los Angeles
Los Angeles, California

Lydia Song
Program Specialist, Mathematics
Orange County Department
    of Education
Costa Mesa, California

Rebecca Valbuena
Language Development
    Specialist
Stanton Elementary School
Glendora, California

iii

School Home CONNECTION

Dear Family,

My class started Unit 5 today. In the next few chapters, I will learn about geometry, patterns, and using position words. Here are vocabulary words and activities for us to share.

Love, _____

Vocabulary Power

Key Math Vocabulary

cone

sphere

cylinder

pyramid

cube

rectangular prism

circle

triangle

rectangle

square

left of the bird   **right of** the kite

Vocabulary Activity

Math on the Move

Provide opportunities to identify figures. Have your child find objects around the home and identify the figures he or she sees on them. Look at doors and windows to find **rectangles** or **squares**. Check in kitchen cupboards for cans shaped like **cylinders**. Can you find examples of each figure listed to the left?

GO ONLINE
Technology
Multimedia Math Glossary link at
www.harcourtschool.com/hspmath

School Home CONNECTION

Remember This
Your child learned about identifying and extending patterns in Kindergarten. Ask your child to circle the bear that comes next in the pattern.

Calendar Activity

February

Sunday	Monday	Tuesday	Wednesday	Thursday	Friday	Saturday
	1	2	3	4	5	6
7	8	9	10	11	12	13
14	15	16	17	18	19	20
21	22	23	24	25	26	27
28						

Review
Have your child use the word *between* to describe February 9.

Practice (after pages 389–390)
Have your child draw a circle around the first day of the month, a triangle around the last day of the month, and a square around today.

Practice (after pages 407–408)
Have your child show a pattern by using two colors to color the dates on the above calendar.

Literature
Look for these books in a library. Ask your child to point out math vocabulary words as you read each book together.

Pattern Fish,
by Trudy Harris,
Greenwillow, 2001.

City Shapes,
by Daniel Jacobs,
Capstone, 2004.

Kitten Castle,
by Mel Friedman and Ellen Weiss,
Kane, 2001.

The Shape of Things,
by Dayle Ann Dodds,
Candlewick, 1996.

READ
Math
Workshop

On the Move

written by Jennifer Earnshaw

In this story you will also and ▸WRITE Math ▸.

 Family Note: This story will help your child review geometric figures.

A

The train car waits for the engine.

Name some figures you see.

Social Studies

What will this train bring?

B

The big truck travels up the road.
Name some figures you see.

Social Studies

What will this truck bring?

C

The ship loads at the dock.

Name some figures you see.

What will this ship bring?

These trucks drive across town.

Name some figures you see.

Social Studies

What will these trucks bring?

E

The airplane arrives at the airport.

Name some figures you see.

Social Studies

What will this airplane bring?

F

Name _____

My Math Story
Literature Activity

Think of another kind of truck that takes goods from one place to another. Draw a picture. Use circles, squares, triangles, or rectangles in your drawing.

Vocabulary Review

circle   triangle

square   rectangle

WRITE Math ▶ Write about your drawing.

_____
- -
_____
_____
- -
_____
_____
- -
_____

G

Name _____

Figure it out

1. Draw an airplane.
Use some triangles and circles in your drawing.

2. Draw a train.
Use some rectangles and circles
in your drawing.

WRITE Math ▶ Choose 2 figures to use
to draw a ship. Write the steps. Draw the ship.

18 Solid and Plane Figures

Theme: In the Water

California Fun Fact

Kayaking is a favorite activity at Mono Lake in California.

Investigate
Kayaks and paddles have curved surfaces. Name another object that has a curved surface.

GO ONLINE **Technology**
Student pages are available in the Student eBook.

The Big Idea Plane and solid figures can be sorted and classified according to their geometric properties.

© Harcourt

Name _____

Show What You Know

Sort by Color, Size, and Shape

Sort by color.
Circle the shape that belongs in the group.

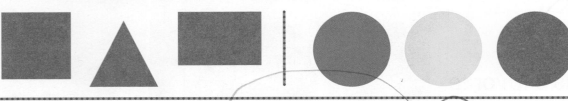

1.

2.

Sort by size.
Mark an X on the object that does not belong.

3.

4.

Sort by shape.
Mark an X on the group in which the shape belongs.

5.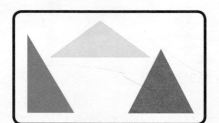

 Family note: This page checks your child's understanding of important concepts and skills needed for success in Chapter 18.

© Harcourt

Name _____

Solid Figures

OBJECTIVE • Identify, describe, and compare solid figures.

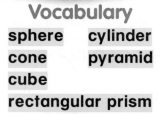

 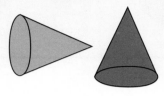 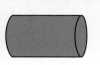

sphere   cone   cylinder

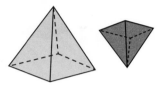 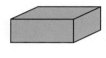

pyramid   rectangular prism   cube

> A cube is a special kind of rectangular prism.

Guided Practice

Circle each cylinder.

1.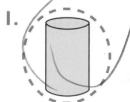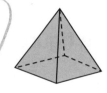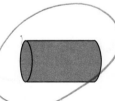

Circle each cone.

2.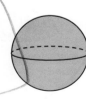

Circle each rectangular prism.

3.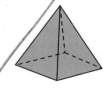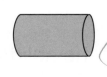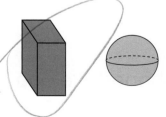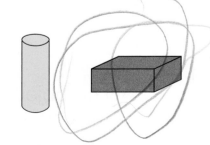

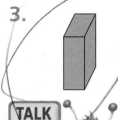 **TALK Math**   How are all cylinders alike? Explain.

© Harcourt

MG 2.2 Classify familiar plane and solid objects by common attributes, such as color, position, shape, size, roundness, or number of corners, and explain which attributes are being used for classification. *also* SDAP 1.1, MR 1.2

Circle each cube.

1.
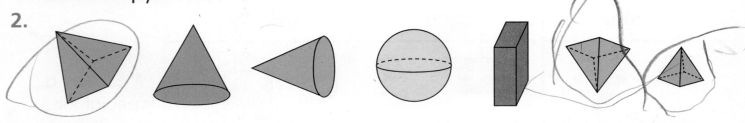

Circle each pyramid.

2.

Circle each sphere.

3.
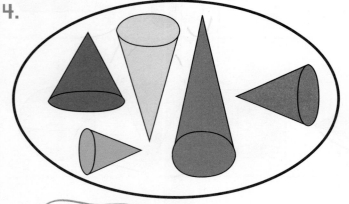

Problem Solving · Reasoning

WRITE Math

Circle the word to tell how these figures are sorted.

4.

cones   pyramids

5.
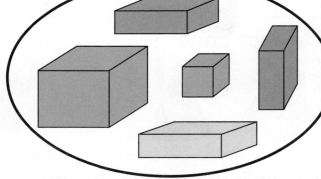

cylinders   rectangular prisms

Draw an object shaped like one of the solids on this page. Write the name of the solid it shows.

TAKE HOME ACTIVITY • Find objects that are shaped like the solids on this page. Have your child identify each object as a sphere, cube, rectangular prism, pyramid, cone, or cylinder.

Name _____

 Sort Solids

OBJECTIVE · Sort solid figures by their flat and curved surfaces.

Vocabulary
curved surface
flat surface

Explore

Some solids have a curved surface.	Some solids have flat surfaces.	Some solids have both curved and flat surfaces.

sphere   cone
  cylinder
	cube pyramid
	  rectangular prism
	  cone cylinder
		cone
		  cylinder

Connect

Use solids.

1. Circle each solid with only flat surfaces.

2. Circle each solid with only a curved surface.

   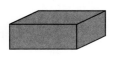

3. Circle each solid with both curved and flat surfaces.

   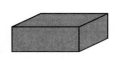

 **TALK Math** How are a cone and a cylinder the same?
How are they different?

MG 2.2 Classify familiar plane and solid objects by common attributes, such as color, position, shape, size, roundness, or number of corners, and explain which attributes are being used for classification. *also* **SDAP 1.1, MR 1.2**

© Harcourt

Color the pictures. Use solids if you need to.

1. I have only a curved surface.
2. I have only flat surfaces.
3. I have both curved and flat surfaces.

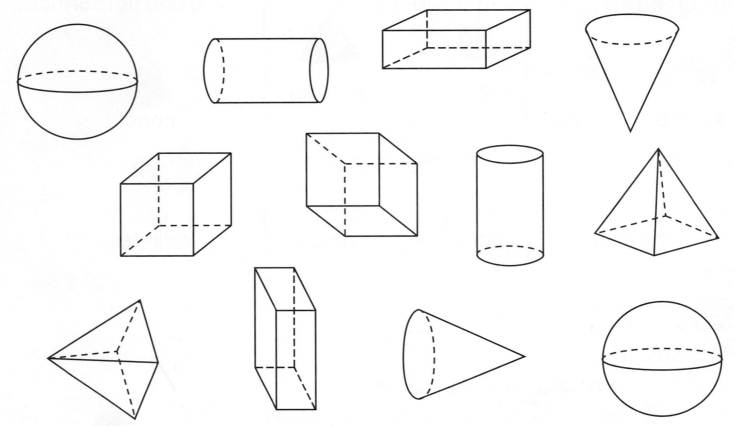

Problem Solving • Visual Thinking ── WRITE Math ▶

4. Sort. Cross out one solid that does not belong.
   Circle the sentence that tells your sorting rule.

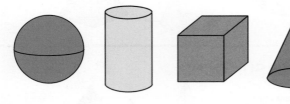

They all have a curved surface.

They all have a flat surface.

 Use the other sorting rule to sort the four solids.
Which solid do you cross out? Explain.

🏠 **TAKE HOME ACTIVITY** • Find objects that are shaped like the solids on this page. Have your child name each figure and tell whether it has curved or flat surfaces.

Classify Solids

OBJECTIVE · Classify solid figures by the number of flat surfaces and corners they have.

Vocabulary
corner
flat surface

 **Explore**

A cube has 6 flat surfaces and 8 **corners**.

flat surface

corner

Connect

Use solids.

1. Circle each solid with 5 corners.

   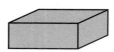

2. Circle each solid with 5 flat surfaces.

   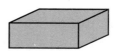

3. Circle each solid with 6 flat surfaces.

   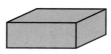

4. Circle each solid with 8 corners.

   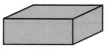

5. Circle each solid with no corners.

   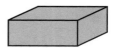

 **TALK Math** How are a rectangular prism and a cube alike?

MG 2.2 Classify familiar plane and solid objects by common attributes, such as color, position, shape, size, roundness, or number of corners, and explain which attributes are being used for classification. *also* SDAP 1.1, MR 1.2

© Harcourt

Practice

Use solids. Write the number of
flat surfaces and corners.

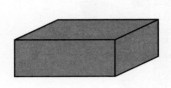

1. This rectangular prism has ___6___ flat surfaces.

2. This rectangular prism has _____ corners.

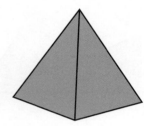

3. This cube has _____ flat surfaces.

4. This cube has _____ corners.

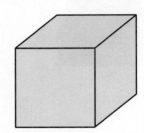

5. This pyramid has _____ flat surfaces.

6. This pyramid has _____ corners.

Problem Solving • Reasoning

WRITE Math

Circle two objects that have the same
number of corners.

7.
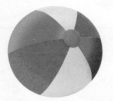  

8.

 Draw something in your classroom that has
8 corners. Write the name of the solid it shows.

TAKE HOME ACTIVITY • Ask your child to count the corners and flat
surfaces on a tissue box. Have him or her tell the name of the solid it shows.

Name _____

 Plane Figures on Solids
OBJECTIVE • Identify plane figures on solids.

Vocabulary
circle
triangle
rectangle
square

Explore

Flat surfaces on solid figures are plane figures.

circle

triangle

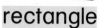
rectangle

square

Connect

Trace around the solid.
Write the name of the figure you drew.

1.

rectangle

2.

_____

3.
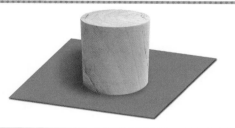
_____

4.
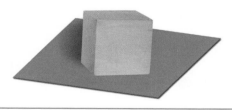
_____

 **TALK Math** What figures can you trace from a pyramid? Explain.

MG 2.1 Identify, describe, and compare triangles, rectangles, squares, and circles, including the faces of three-dimensional objects. *also* MR1.2

Circle the objects you could trace to make the figure.

1.

2.

3.

4.

Problem Solving • Reasoning — WRITE Math

Connect the dots to draw each figure.
Color the square 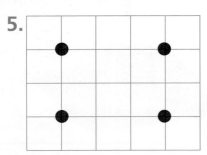. Color the triangle 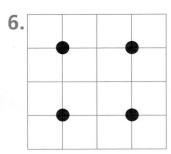.
Color the rectangle 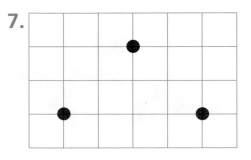.

5.

6.

7.

 Describe what you notice about the square.

TAKE HOME ACTIVITY • Have your child trace the flat surfaces of solid objects, such as small boxes or cans, on a sheet of paper. Ask him or her to name each figure he or she traced.

Name _____

Sort Plane Figures
OBJECTIVE · Identify and sort plane figures.

Vocabulary
rectangle
square
circle
triangle

Learn

A square is a special kind of rectangle.

   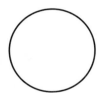

rectangle   square   circle   triangle

Guided Practice

1. Color each circle .

2. Color each square 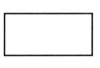.

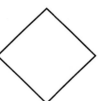

3. Color each rectangle .

 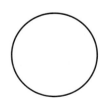

TALK Math  Which figures are triangles? Explain.

 **MG 2.2** Classify familiar plane and solid objects by common attributes, such as color, position, shape, size, roundness, or number of corners, and explain which attributes are being used for classification. *also* **SDAP 1.1, MG 2.1, MR 1.2**

1. Color ○ . 2. Color □ . 3. Color △ .

Problem Solving · Reasoning ——— WRITE Math ▶

5. Draw a house. Use at least one circle, one triangle, and two different rectangles.

 Describe the two different rectangles you drew.

🏠 **TAKE HOME ACTIVITY ·** Have your child identify objects around the house that are shaped like rectangles, circles, triangles, or squares.

HANDS ON

Classify Plane Figures

OBJECTIVE · Classify plane figures by the number of sides and corners they have.

Vocabulary
side
corner

Explore

Some figures have straight sides and corners.

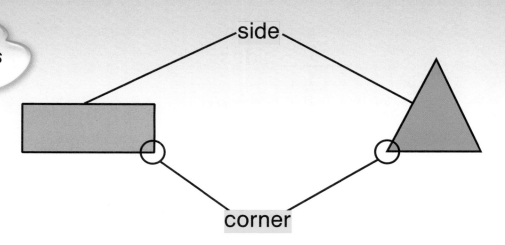

side

corner

Connect

Use plane figures to sort. Write the number of straight sides and corners.

	Plane Figure	Straight Sides	Corners
1.			
2.			
3.			
4.			

TALK Math  Look at the chart. What is the same?

MG 2.2 Classify familiar plane and solid objects by common attributes, such as color, position, shape, size, roundness, or number of corners, and explain which attributes are being used for classification. *also* **SDAP 1.1, MR 1.2**

© Harcourt

Practice

Use  to trace each straight side.
Use  to circle each corner.
Write the number of sides and corners.

1. 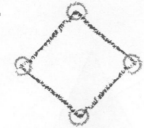   4 sides
   4 corners

2. _____ sides
   _____ corners

3. _____ sides
   _____ corners

4. _____ sides
   _____ corners

5. _____ sides
   _____ corners

6. _____ sides
   _____ corners

Problem Solving • Visual Thinking — WRITE Math ▶

Draw a picture to solve.

7. I am a figure with 3 straight sides and 3 corners.

8. I am a figure with 4 straight sides and 4 corners.

 Look at Exercise 8. Draw a different figure to solve the problem. Explain.

 TAKE HOME ACTIVITY • Have your child draw a square, rectangle, and triangle. For each figure, have him or her show you the sides and corners and tell how many of each there are.

392 three hundred ninety-two

Problem Solving Workshop
Strategy • Use Logical Reasoning
OBJECTIVE • Solve problems by using the strategy *use logical reasoning*.

Learn the Strategy

You can think like a math
detective to solve problems.

I do not have a curved surface.
I have fewer than 5 sides.
I have only 3 corners.
Which figure am I?

Use Logical Reasoning

Use the clues. Cross off each figure that
does not match. Circle the figure that is left.

Clue 1 I do not have a curved surface.
The ⬤ has a curved surface.

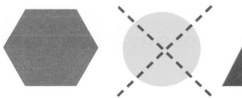

Clue 2 I have fewer than 5 sides.
The ⬡ has more than 5 sides.

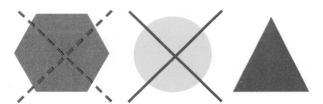

Clue 3 I have 3 corners.
A ▲ has 3 corners.

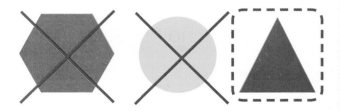

TALK Math Explain how your answer matches each clue.

MG 2.2 Classify familiar plane and solid objects by common attributes, such as color, position, shape, size, roundness, or number of corners, and explain which attributes are being used for classification. *also* SDAP 1.1, MR 1.1, MR 1.2, MR 2.1, MR 2.2

Chapter 18 • Lesson 7
three hundred ninety-three 393

© Harcourt

Use the Strategy • Use Logical Reasoning

I have a curved surface.
I have two flat surfaces.
I have no corners.
Which figure am I ?

Read to Understand

What do you know?
Read each clue.

Plan

Use picture clues to solve the problem.
Cross off each figure that does not match.
Circle the figure that is left.

Solve

Find the figure that matches all the clues.

The ◻ does not have a curved surface.

The △ has only one flat surface.

The ▮ has no corners.

Check

Explain how your answer matches each clue.

© Harcourt

Name _____

Problem Solving Strategy Practice

Cross off figures that do not match the clues.
Circle the figure that is left.

1. I have straight sides. I have more than 3 corners. My sides do not all have the same length. Which figure am I?

2. I have no curved surface. I have more than 5 flat surfaces. All of my flat surfaces are the same size. Which figure am I?

3. I have a curved surface. I have no flat surfaces. I have no corners. Which figure am I?

4. **Try Your Own Problem**

   My sides all have the same

   length. I have more than ____

   sides. I have ____ corners.
   Which figure am I?

Technology
Use Harcourt Mega Math,
Shapes Ahoy!, *Ship Shapes*, Level O.

© Harcourt

Mixed Strategy Practice

Choose a way to solve each problem.
Show your work.

1. Jeremy sees 9 ducks.
Paula sees 8 more ducks.
How many ducks do Jeremy
and Paula see?

WRITE Math ▶ Write or draw to explain.

duck

_____ ducks

2. There are 2 oars in each
boat. How many oars
are there in 4 boats?

oar

_____ oars

3. Noah counted 11 turtles on
a log. 5 turtles went into the
pond. How many turtles stayed
on the log?

turtle

_____ turtles

4. I have corners. I have fewer
than 6 sides. My sides do not
all have the same length.
Which figure am I?

© Harcourt

Name _____

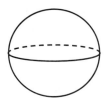 **Extra Practice**

1. Color the rectangular prism .

2. Color the solid that has only a curved surface 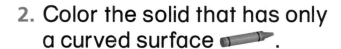.

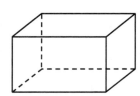

Use solids. Write the number of flat surfaces and corners.

3. This cube has _____ flat surfaces.

4. This cube has _____ corners.

5. Circle the objects you could trace to make the figure.

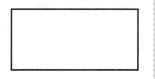     

6. Color each triangle .

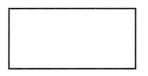 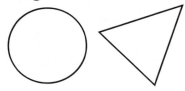 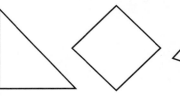

7. Use to trace each straight side.
   Use to circle each corner.
   Write the number of sides and corners.

   _____ sides

   _____ corners

Problem Solving

Cross off figures that do not match the clues. Circle the figure that is left.

8. I have straight sides.
   I have only 3 corners.
   Which figure am I?

 Technology
Use Mega Math CD-ROM, Shapes Ahoy!, *Undersea 3D*, Levels F, G.
ROM

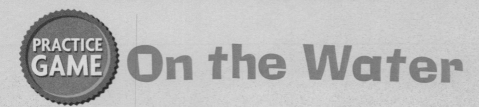

PRACTICE GAME
On the Water

Play with a partner.

1. Put your ♟ on START.
2. Spin the 🕐. Move your ♟ that many spaces.
3. Look at the figure. Tell how many corners. Tell how many sides.
4. The other player uses figures to check. If you are not correct, lose a turn.
5. The first player to get to END wins.

You will need
- ♟ ♟
- 🕐
- ▲ ■ ● ▮

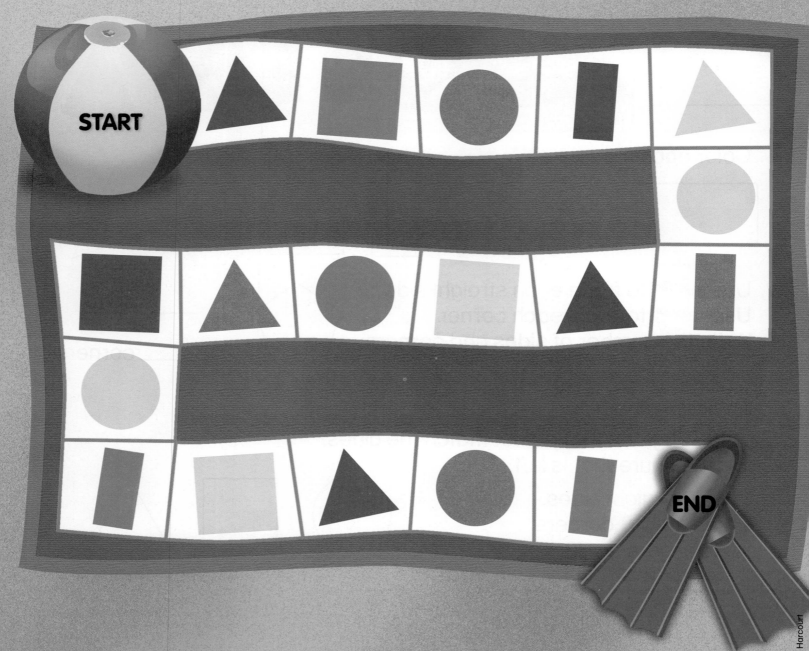

Name _____

Vocabulary ————————————————————

1. Color the cube . (MG 2.2)
2. Color the cone . (MG 2.2)

Concepts and Skills ————————————————

Use solids. Write the number of
flat surfaces and corners. (MG 2.2)

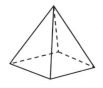

3. This pyramid has _____ flat surfaces.

4. This pyramid has _____ corners.

5. Circle the objects you could trace to make the figure. (MG 2.1)

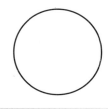

6. Color each rectangle . (MG 2.2)

  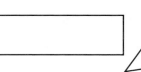 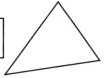

7. Trace each side. Circle the corners. (MG 2.2)
   Write the number of sides and corners.

_____ sides   _____ corners

Problem Solving ————————————————

Cross off figures that do not match the
clues. Circle the figure that is left. (MG 2.2)

8. I have no curved surfaces.
   I have 5 flat surfaces.
   Four surfaces are the same shape.
   Which figure am I?

Go ONLINE Technology
Use *Online Assessment*.

Enrich • Figures and Solids
Is It the Same?

How are the figures the same?

Each figure has four sides.

Reasoning

Draw a line to match each sentence with the group it describes.

1. Each figure has a curved surface. •

   Each figure has 4 corners. •

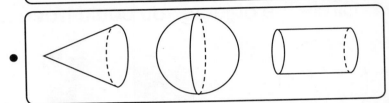

2. Each figure has 3 sides. •

   You can trace each figure to make a circle. •

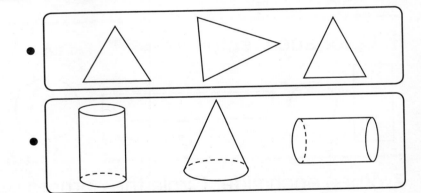

Try Your Own

3. Draw 3 figures that are the same in some way. Write a rule that describes how the figures are the same.

TALK Math Look at Exercise 2. What is another rule for the top group of figures? Explain.

Name —————————————————————

Choose the best answer for questions 1–5.

1. **Which is a way to make 8?** (NS 1.3)

    (A) 10 − 2   (C) 6 + 1

    (B) 5 − 3   (D) 8 − 5

2. **Which symbol completes the sentence?** (0—π NS 1.2)

    21 ◯ 19

    (A) >   (B) =   (C) <   (D) −

3. **How many** **are equal to one** **?** (NS 1.5)

    (A) 1   (B) 5   (C) 10   (D) 25

4. **Which solid has a curved surface?** (MG 2.2)

    (A)   (B)   (C)   (D)

5. **How many corners does this solid have?** (MG 2.2)

    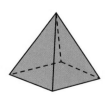

    (A) 3   (B) 5   (C) 6   (D) 8

Choose the best answer for questions 6-8.

6. Which plane figure can you trace from a cylinder? (MG 2.1)

Ⓐ ○

Ⓒ ▢

Ⓑ ▭

Ⓓ △

7. Which is a rectangle? (MG 2.1)

Ⓐ

Ⓒ

Ⓑ

Ⓓ

8. Which plane figure has 4 sides and 4 corners? (MG 2.2)

Ⓐ circle

Ⓒ triangle

Ⓑ cube

Ⓓ square

WRITE Math ▶ Explain your answer for questions 9-11.

Use the table to answer the questions. (MG 1.2)

At the Pool		
Activity	Start	End
swim lessons	9:30	11:00
pool races	11:00	11:30
water games	12:00	1:00

9. Which activity starts after pool races?

_____

_ _ _ _ _ _ _ _ _ _ _ _ _ _ _ _ _ _ _.

_____

10. Which activity last the longest time?

_____

_ _ _ _ _ _ _ _ _ _ _ _ _ _ _ _ _ _ _.

_____

Cross off figures that do not match the clues.
Circle the figure that is left. (MG 2.2, MR 2.2)

11. This figure has 8 corners. It has 6 flat surfaces.
All the flat surfaces are **not** the same size.
Which is the figure?

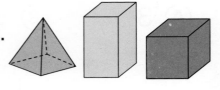

CHAPTER 19 Patterns

Theme: On Land

California Fun Fact

These footprints are at Pismo Beach State Park in California. A beach is a sandy area of land by the water.

Investigate

Describe the pattern of the footprints.

GO ONLINE

Technology
Student pages are available in the Student eBook.

The Big Idea Patterns are found in physical and geometric situations and in numbers.

Name _____

 Show What You Know

Identify Patterns

Read the pattern. Place bears to identify the pattern.
Color the pattern.

1.

2.

Read the pattern. Place shapes to identify the pattern.
Trace and color the pattern.

3.

4.

 Family note: This page checks your child's understanding of important concepts and skills needed for success in Chapter 19.

© Harcourt

Algebra: Pattern Units
OBJECTIVE • Identify, describe, and extend pattern units.

Vocabulary
repeating pattern
pattern unit

A repeating pattern has a group that repeats over and over.

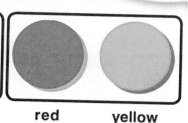
A group that repeats is called a **pattern unit**.

| red | yellow | red | yellow | red | yellow |

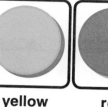 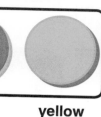

Connect

Use ⬤ or 🎲 🎲 🎲 to copy the repeating pattern.
Circle each pattern unit.

1.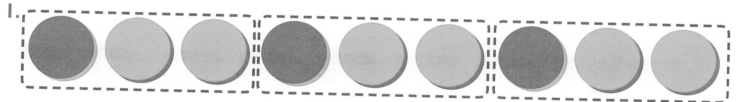

2.

3.

4.

 **TALK Math**
How do you find a pattern unit? Explain.

SDAP 2.1 Describe, extend, and explain ways to get to a next element in simple repeating patterns (e.g., rhythmic, numeric, color, and shape).

Chapter 19 • Lesson 1

Circle the first pattern unit.

1.

2.

3.

4.

Problem Solving · Reasoning ═══ ⟩WRITE Math ▶

5. Draw 3 ♥ and 6 ♥ to show a repeating pattern.
The pattern unit should repeat three times.
Circle the first pattern unit.

 How do you know that your drawing shows
a repeating pattern? Explain.

 TAKE HOME ACTIVITY • Ask your child to find a repeating pattern in
wrapping paper, clothing, or elsewhere and to identify the pattern unit.

© Harcourt

Algebra: Color Patterns

OBJECTIVE · Identify, describe, and extend repeating color patterns.

Vocabulary
pattern unit

Learn

This color pattern is made using one figure with different colors.

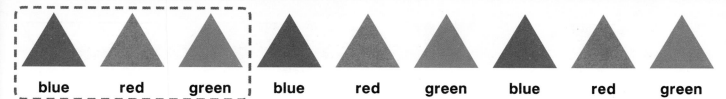

| blue | red | green | blue | red | green | blue | red | green |

pattern unit

Guided Practice

Two pattern units are shown. Circle the first pattern unit. Color to continue the pattern.

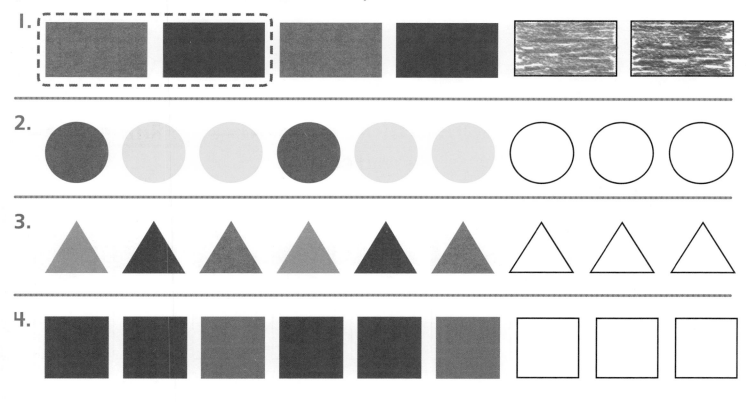

1.

2.

3.

4.

TALK Math

How can you change one circle to make this a repeating pattern?

© Harcourt

SDAP 2.1 Describe, extend, and explain ways to get to a next element in simple repeating patterns (e.g., rhythmic, numeric, color, and shape).

Independent Practice

Circle the first pattern unit.
Color to continue the pattern.

1.

2.

3.

4.

5.

Problem Solving • Application

WRITE Math ▶

6. Use the same two colors. Show a color pattern with a different pattern unit.

How are the pattern units different? Explain.

 TAKE HOME ACTIVITY • Have your child use crayons to draw two different repeating color patterns. Ask him or her to explain the difference between the patterns.

© Harcourt

Name _____

Algebra: Shape Patterns

OBJECTIVE • Identify, describe, and extend repeating shape patterns.

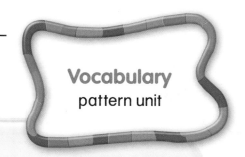
 **Learn**

The first pattern unit is circle, triangle, triangle.

Guided Practice

Circle the first pattern unit.
Draw and color what comes next.

 **TALK Math**

How are these pattern units alike and different? Explain.

© Harcourt

SDAP 2.1 Describe, extend, and explain ways to get to a next element in simple repeating patterns (e.g., rhythmic, numeric, color, and shape).

Independent Practice

Find a pattern unit.
Draw and color what comes next.

1.

2.

3.

4.

5.

Problem Solving • Reasoning ─── ▌WRITE Math ⟩

Draw and color the missing figure in
each repeating pattern.

7.

8.

Look at Exercise 8. Explain how
you decide what is missing.

TAKE HOME ACTIVITY • Have your child draw
a repeating pattern using circles and squares.

410 four hundred ten

© Harcourt

Algebra: Number Patterns

OBJECTIVE • Identify, describe, and extend repeating number patterns.

Learn

I comes next.

| 1 | 2 | 3 | 1 | 2 | 3 | 1 | 2 | 3 |

Guided Practice

Circle the first pattern unit. Write the next number.

1. [1 2] 1 2 1 2 1 2 1 2 ____ 1

2. | 1 | 3 | 5 | 1 | 3 | 5 | 1 | 3 | 5 | ____

3. 2 2 4 2 2 4 2 2 4 2 ____

4. | 3 | 4 | 3 | 4 | 3 | 4 | 3 | 4 | 3 | 4 | 3 | ____

5. 5 4 4 5 4 4 5 4 4 5 4 ____

6. | 4 | 3 | 2 | 4 | 3 | 2 | 4 | 3 | 2 | 4 | 3 | ____

TALK Math  Look at Exercise 4. How did you decide what number comes next?

© Harcourt

O—π SDAP 2.1 Describe, extend, and explain ways to get to a next element in simple repeating patterns (e.g., rhythmic, numeric, color, and shape).

Chapter 19 • Lesson 4
four hundred eleven 411

Independent Practice

Circle the first pattern unit. Continue the pattern.

1. (4 1) 4 1 4 1 4 1   __4__ __1__

2. 1 2 2 1 2 2 1 2 2   ____ ____

3. 5 4 3 5 4 3 5 4 3   ____ ____

4. 2 3 2 3 2 3 2   ____ ____

5. 4 4 5 4 4 5 4 4 5 4   ____ ____

6. 3 1 2 3 1 2 3 1 2 3   ____ ____

7. 5 5 1 5 5 1 5 5   ____ ____

Problem Solving • Reasoning

WRITE Math

8. Circle the mistake in the pattern.
Write the correct pattern.

1   1   2   1   2   2   1   1   2

____ ____ ____ ____ ____ ____ ____ ____ ____

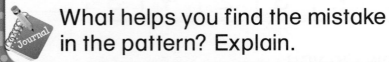

What helps you find the mistake
in the pattern? Explain.

 TAKE HOME ACTIVITY • Have your child write repeating number patterns using 3s and 4s. Ask them to explain their patterns and to identify the next number.

© Harcourt

Algebra: Rhythmic Patterns

OBJECTIVE • Identify, describe, and extend repeating rhythmic patterns.

Learn

This pattern is made using sounds.

snap   clap   clap   snap   clap   clap   snap   clap   clap

Guided Practice

Find a pattern unit.
Circle what comes next.

1.

   snap   snap   tap   snap   snap   tap   snap   snap   tap

   ⌐snap¬   tap

2.

   tap   clap   tap   clap   tap   clap   tap   clap

   clap   tap

3.

   clap   snap   tap   clap   snap   tap   clap   snap   tap

   clap   snap

TALK Math Look at Exercise 2. How is it like this pattern?

● ■ ● ■ ● ■

 SDAP 2.1 Describe, extend, and explain ways to get to a next element in simple repeating patterns (e.g., rhythmic, numeric, color, and shape).

Chapter 19 • Lesson 5

Independent Practice

Find a pattern unit.
Circle what comes next.

1. tap tap snap tap tap snap tap tap snap   snap [tap]

2. snap clap snap clap snap clap snap clap   clap snap

3. clap snap tap clap snap tap clap snap tap   clap tap

Problem Solving • Application ═══ WRITE Math

4. Find the pattern unit.
   Draw ● and ■ to show the same pattern.

clap tap tap clap tap tap clap tap tap

How are the patterns alike
and different? Explain.

 TAKE HOME ACTIVITY • Have your child make up a repeating pattern using
claps, snaps, or taps and teach it to you. Perform the pattern together.

© Harcourt

Problem Solving Workshop
Strategy • Find a Pattern
OBJECTIVE • Solve problems by using the strategy *find a pattern*.

Andy is making a repeating pattern with tiles.
Some tiles are missing.
How many tiles does he need?

Read to Understand

What do you want to find out?
Circle the question.

Plan

How can you solve the problem?
Use picture clues.
Find a repeating pattern in the tiles.

Solve

Color the missing tiles to show the pattern.
Write how many tiles Andy needs.

$\dfrac{2}{3}$ ■ □

Check

Explain why your answer is correct.

© Harcourt

SDAP 2.1 Describe, extend, and explain ways to get to a next element in simple repeating patterns (e.g. rhythmic, numeric, color, and shape). *also* **MR 1.1, MR 1.2, MR 2.1, MR 2.2**

Problem Solving Strategy Practice

Color the missing tiles to show the repeating
pattern. Write how many tiles are needed.

1.

_____

_____

2.

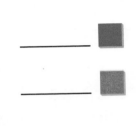

_____

_____

3.

_____

_____

4. **Try Your Own Problem**

Use 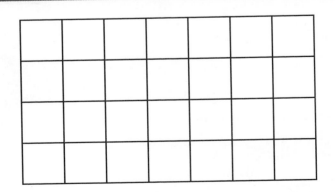 and .

Color a tile pattern.

Leave 4 tiles empty.

Trade with a classmate.

Solve.

© Harcourt

 Extra Practice

1. Use 🎲 and 🎲 to copy the repeating pattern. Circle each pattern unit.

2. Circle the first pattern unit. Color to continue the pattern.

3. Circle the first pattern unit. Draw and color what comes next.

4. Circle the first pattern unit. Continue the pattern.

$$3 \quad 4 \quad 5 \quad 3 \quad 4 \quad 5 \quad 3 \quad 4 \quad 5 \quad \underline{\quad} \ \underline{\quad}$$

5. Find a pattern unit. Circle what comes next.

clap snap snap clap snap snap clap snap snap | clap snap

Problem Solving

6. Color the missing tiles to show the repeating pattern. Write how many tiles are needed.

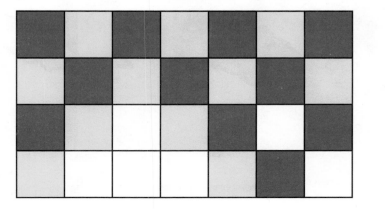

_____ ■

_____ ▢

Technology
Use Mega Math CD-ROM, Shapes Ahoy!,
Ship Shapes, Level C, D.

Tile Pattern Pickup

Play with a partner.

1. Put your 🗿 on START.
2. Spin the 🔴. Move that number of spaces. Look at the space you are on.
3. Take that number and color of tiles.
4. When you reach the END, make a pattern with your tiles. Use as many tiles as you can.
5. The player who uses the most tiles in a pattern with no mistakes is the winner.

You will need
- 🗿🗿
- 🔴
- 15 ⬛
- 15 ⬛
- 15 ⬜

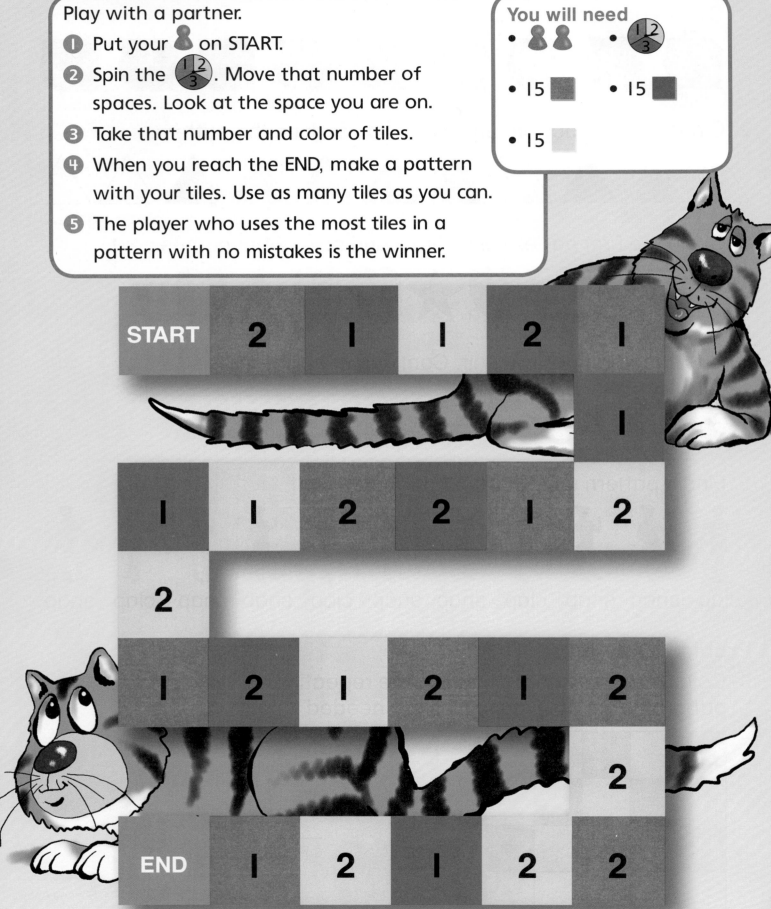

START	2	1	1	2	1

1	1	2	2	1	2

1	2	1	2	1	2

END	1	2	1	2	2

Chapter Review/Test

Vocabulary

1. Circle the group that shows a repeating **pattern** . (O—¬ SDAP 2.1)

2. Circle the **pattern unit** 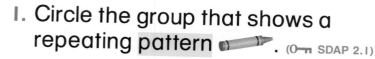. (O—¬ SDAP 2.1)

Concepts and Skills

3. Find a pattern unit. Color to continue the pattern. (O—¬ SDAP 2.1)

4. Find a pattern unit. Draw and color what comes next. (O—¬ SDAP 2.1)

5. Circle the first pattern unit. Continue the pattern. (O—¬ SDAP 2.1)

4   2   2   4   2   2   4   2   _____

6. Find a pattern unit. Circle what comes next. (O—¬ SDAP 2.1)

clap   clap   tap   clap   clap   tap   clap   clap   tap   clap   tap

Problem Solving

7. Color the missing tiles. Write how many tiles are needed to finish each pattern. (O—¬ SDAP 2.1)

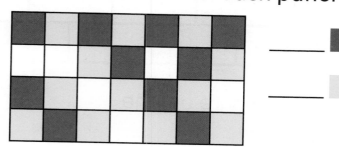

_____ ■

_____ ▢

Use *Online Assessment.*

Enrich • Patterns
Building Walls

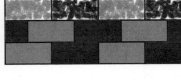 is using a pattern to build a wall.
Circle the mistake in the wall on the left.
Use the pattern to color the wall on the right.

HINT
Find the mistake in the pattern. Color the missing bricks to correct the pattern.

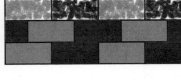

Reasoning

1. Circle the mistake in the pattern on the left.
   Use the pattern to color the wall on the right.

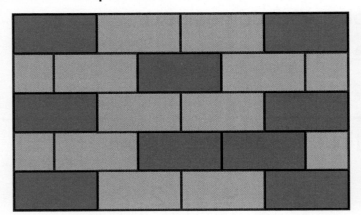

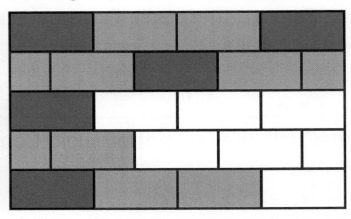

Try Your Own

2. Color a pattern with a mistake.
   Circle the mistake in the pattern.
   Color the correct pattern.

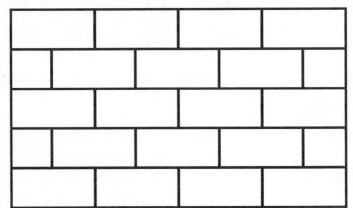

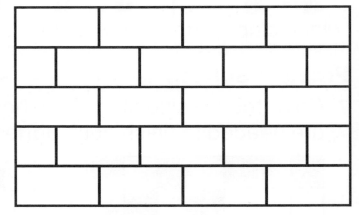

 Look at Exercise 1. How do you figure out the correct pattern? Explain.

Chapter 19

© Harcourt

Name _____

Choose the best answer for questions 1–4.

1. What are the missing numbers? (O−n NS 2.4)

15, _____, 25, 30, _____, _____

Ⓐ 16, 31, 32   Ⓒ 20, 35, 40

Ⓑ 20, 30, 50   Ⓓ 20, 35, 45

---

2. What is the difference? (O−n NS 2.1)

$$9 \atop {+\,8} \atop \overline{17}$$ $$17 \atop {-\,8} \atop $$

Ⓐ 11   Ⓑ 7   Ⓒ 8   Ⓓ 9

---

3. What is the first pattern unit? (O−n SDAP 2.1)

Ⓐ   Ⓒ

Ⓑ   Ⓓ

---

4. What comes next in the pattern? (O−n SDAP 2.1)

Ⓐ   Ⓑ   Ⓒ   Ⓓ

Choose the best answer for questions 5-6.

5. What comes next in the pattern? (O—n SDAP 2.1)

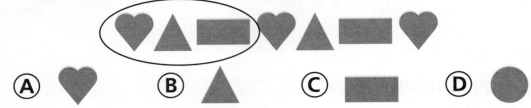

(A) ♥   (B) ▲   (C) ▬   (D) ●

6. What comes next in the pattern? (O—n SDAP 2.1)

tap snap clap tap snap clap tap snap clap tap snap

(A) tap   (B) snap   (C) clap   (D) clap snap

WRITE Math ▸ Explain your answer for questions 7-8.

Cross off figures that do not match the clues.

Circle the figure that is left. (MG 2.2)

7. This figure has less than 4 sides. It has no corners. When you trace a cone, you draw this figure.

Which is the figure?

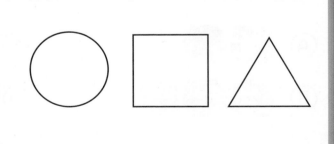

8. Write how many tiles are needed to finish the pattern. (O—n SDAP 2.1)

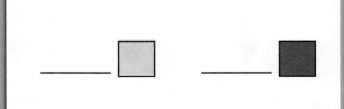

© Harcourt

CHAPTER

20 Spatial Sense

Theme: In the Sky

California Fun Fact

There are many hot air balloon festivals and fairs in California. These hot air balloons are flying over Siskiyou County in northern California.

Investigate

Look at the picture. Use position words to describe one of the hot air balloons.

GO ONLINE Technology
Student pages are available in the Student eBook.

The Big Idea Shapes can be described in terms of their location in a plane or in space.

Show What You Know

Above and Below

1. Place a red cube above the bear. Draw the cube.

2. Place a blue cube below the bear. Draw the cube.

Sort Plane Figures

3. Color each rectangle  .

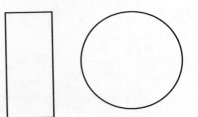  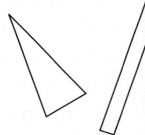

4. Color each triangle 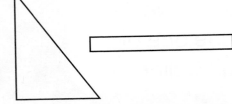 .

 Family note: This page checks your child's understanding of important concepts and skills needed for success in Chapter 20.

Name _____

Position Words

OBJECTIVE • Use position words to identify, describe, and arrange objects.

Vocabulary

up	down
above	below
far	near
right of	left of
in front of	behind
next to	

Learn

Position words tell where objects are.

left of the bird
above the rabbit

behind the bird

up

in front of the cloud
right of the kite

far from the tree
below the kite

near the tree

down

next to the tree

Guided Practice

Use the picture to solve. Circle the answer.

1. The is to the **right of** the .
   What is to the **right of** the ?

2. The is to the **left of** the .
   What is to the **left of** the ?

3. The is **behind** the .
   What is **behind** the ?

4. The is **far** from the .
   What is **far** from the ?

 Find a desk and a chair in your classroom.
Use position words to tell where the chair is.

© Harcourt

MG 2.4 Arrange and describe objects in space by proximity, position, and direction (e.g., near, far, below, above, up, down, behind, in front of, next to, left or right of).

Independent Practice

Read the directions.
Write **A**, **B**, **C**, and **D** to place the pictures.

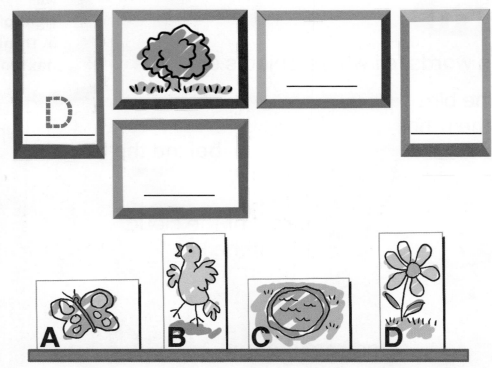

1. Place the 🌼 to the **left of** the 🌳 .

2. Place the 🪹 **below** the 🌳 .

3. Place the 🦋 **next to** the 🌳 .

4. Place the 🐤 to the **right of** the 🦋 .

Problem Solving · Reasoning ———— WRITE Math ▶

5. Circle the true statements.

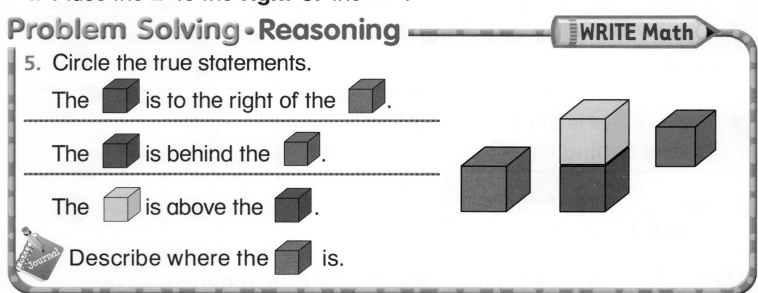

The ⬛ is to the right of the ⬛ .

The ⬛ is behind the ⬛ .

The ⬜ is above the ⬛ .

Describe where the ⬛ is.

TAKE HOME ACTIVITY • Arrange four or five small toys or other objects on a table. Have your child use words such as *below, left,* and *behind* to describe the position of one of the toys. Use the clues to guess which object he or she is describing. Take turns describing positions and identifying toys.

© Harcourt

Name _____

Follow Directions

OBJECTIVE • Use position words to follow directions about location.

Learn

Position words help you find and place objects.

Guided Practice

Use the picture to solve. Draw to show the answer.

1. The 🔥 is **next to** the 🌳. Draw a boy **next to** the 🔲.

2. The ☁ is **behind** the ✈. Draw a ball **behind** the 🌳.

3. The ◯ is **above** the 🎈. Draw a kite **above** the 🔥.

4. The ☁ is to the **right of** the ◯.

   Draw a dog to the **right of** the 🧍.

TALK Math What objects are far from the tree?
What objects are near the tree? Explain.

© Harcourt

Independent Practice

Follow the directions. Use the picture.

1. Color the animal to the **left of** the _____. Use _____.

_____

2. Color the animal **below** the _____. Use _____.

_____

3. Color the animal **in front of** the 🌲. Use _____.

_____

4. Color the animal **up** the 🌲. Use _____.

_____

5. Color the animal **near** the 🪑. Use _____.

 TAKE HOME ACTIVITY • Choose a "mystery" object in a room. Have your child ask a series of *yes/no* questions about the position of the object, such as "Is it *above* the sofa?" or "Is it to the *left of* the lamp?" until he or she can identify the object.

Name _____

Give Directions

OBJECTIVE · Give directions, using the relative position of objects in relation to other objects.

Learn

Guided Practice

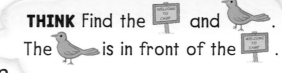

THINK Find the 🪧 and 🐦. The 🐦 is in front of the 🪧.

Use the picture. Circle the correct position word to complete each sentence.

1. The 🐦 is _____ the 🪧.	above	(in front of)
2. The ⚾ is to the _____ the ⛺.	left of	right of
3. The 🚤 is _____ the ▥.	behind	below
4. The 🎒 is _____ the ⬭.	near	far from
5. The 🦝 is _____ the 🌳.	next to	up

TALK Math Name two objects in the picture that are near each other. Explain.

© Harcourt

MG 2.3 Give and follow directions about location. *also* MG 2.4

Independent Practice

Circle every figure that makes the statement true.

There can be more than one answer.

1. The _____ is **next to** the ● .

2. The _____ is **above** the ▲ .

3. The _____ is to the **left of** the ● .

4. The _____ is **below** the ▬ .

Problem Solving • Reasoning ——— WRITE Math ▶

Use the words from 1–4. Complete each sentence.

5. The ■ is _____ the ○ .

6. The ▲ is _____ the ■ .

7. The ▲ is _____ the ▲ .

Use different words to describe the ▲ .

 TAKE HOME ACTIVITY • Ask your child to draw a picture that arranges three figures with different shapes or colors. Without showing you the picture, ask your child to give directions for drawing the same picture. Then compare the results.

Name _____

Problem Solving Workshop
Strategy • Use Logical Reasoning

OBJECTIVE • Solve problems by using the strategy *use logical reasoning.*

Sara paints a (circle) above a (triangle.) She paints a (square) to the left of the (circle.) Which painting is Sara's?

Read to Understand

What clues do you have? Circle the names of the figures Sara paints. Underline the position words.

Plan

Compare and contrast the clues to each painting to help you solve the problem.

Solve

Cross out the paintings that do not match the clues. Circle Sara's painting.

  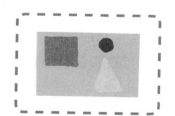

This circle is below the triangle.

This square is to the right of the circle.

This painting matches all the clues.

Check

How does your answer match the clues? Explain.

MG 2.4 Arrange and describe objects in space by proximity, position, and direction (e.g., near, far, below, above, up, down, behind, in front of, next to, left or right of). *also* MG 2.1, MG 2.3, MR 1.1, MR 1.2, MR 2.1

© Harcourt

Problem Solving Strategy Practice

Cross out the paintings that
do not match the clues.
Circle the answer.

1. Jim paints a square
   below a circle.
   He paints a triangle
   below the square.
   Which painting is Jim's?

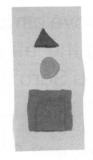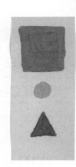

2. Val paints a triangle
   below a circle.
   She paints a square to
   the left of the triangle.
   Which painting is Val's?

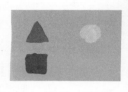

3. Ty paints a square
   next to a circle.
   He paints a triangle
   far from the square.
   Which painting is Ty's?

4. **Try Your Own Problem**
   Ann paints a circle
   _____ the triangle.
   She paints a square
   _____ the triangle.
   Which painting is Ann's?

 TAKE HOME ACTIVITY • Draw three different arrangements of circle, square, and triangle on separate sheets of paper. Give your child clues about the relative positions of the shapes in one of the pictures, using words such as *above* and *to the right of*. Have your child identify the picture being described and explain the choice.

© Harcourt

Name _____

🐻 Extra Practice

Use the picture. Follow the directions.

1. Color the fish to the **right of** the  .

2. Color the fish to the **left of** the .

3. Color the fish **below** the .

Circle the figure that makes the statement true.

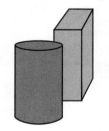 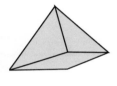 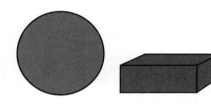

4. The _____ is **in front of** the .

5. The _____ is **next to** the .

6. The _____ is **near** the .

Problem Solving

Cross out the paintings that
do not match the clues.
Circle the answer.

7. Mia paints a square below a circle.
   She paints a triangle to the right of
   the square. Which painting is Mia's?

 Technology
Use Mega Math CD-ROM, Shapes Ahoy!,
Undersea 3D, Level G.

© Harcourt

PRACTICE GAME

Positional Bingo

Play with a partner.

1. One player uses ⬤. The other player uses ⬤.

2. Spin . Choose a space in that color on your game board.

3. Spin 🔘. Move 1 space in that direction from the color space. Cover the space with a counter.

4. If you can not move in that direction, do not cover a space.

5. The first player to get 3 counters in a row wins.

You will need
- 🔘 • 🔘(up/down/left/right)
- • 9 ⬤ • 9 ⬤

Player 1 ▸   Player 2 ▸

Chapter Review/Test

Vocabulary

1. Circle the duck to the **right of the** . Use . (MG 2.4)

2. Circle the duck to the **left of the** . Use . (MG 2.4)

3. Circle the duck **next to** the . Use . (MG 2.4)

Concepts and Skills

Circle the figure that makes the statement true.

4. The _____ is **above** the _____. (MG 2.3)

5. The _____ is **below** the _____. (MG 2.3)

6. The _____ is **far from** the _____. (MG 2.3)

Problem Solving

Cross out the paintings that do not match the clues. Circle the answer. (MG 2.4)

7. Joe paints a square to the right of a circle.
   He paints a triangle to the right of the square.
   Which painting is Joe's?

Technology
Use *Online* Assessment.

Enrich • Positional Words
Treasure Hunt

Max and Pat are having a treasure hunt.
Max hid a cup. He gave Pat these clues
to help her find the cup.

The cup is near books. It is
in front of something square.
It is to the right of the toys.

Use the clues. Draw an X where Max hid the cup.

Reasoning

1. Use the clues. Draw an X where the cup is hidden.

The cup is below the salt.
It is to the left of two
rectangular prisms. It is
to the right of the peas.

Try Your Own

2. Draw a place in your classroom where you
   could hide a cup. Then write clues that
   would help someone find it.

_____

_____

_____

_____

_____

TALK Math Look at Exercise 2. What words give
clues for where the cup is hidden? Explain.

© Harcourt

Unit Review/Test
Chapters 18–20

Choose the best answer for questions 1–5.

1. How many flat surfaces does this solid have? (MG 2.2)

Ⓐ 0   Ⓑ 1   Ⓒ 2   Ⓓ 3

2. What is the first pattern unit? (O—ㄲ SDAP 2.1)

4 1 2 4 1 2 4 1 2

Ⓐ 1 2   Ⓒ 2 4 1

Ⓑ 1 2 4   Ⓓ 4 1 2

3. What comes next in the pattern? (O—ㄲ SDAP 2.1)

snap clap clap snap clap clap snap clap clap snap

Ⓐ snap

Ⓑ tap

Ⓒ clap

Ⓓ  clap snap

4. What is behind the **?** (MG 2.4)

Ⓐ

Ⓑ

Ⓒ

Ⓓ

5. What is next to the **?** (MG 2.4)

Ⓐ    Ⓑ    Ⓒ    Ⓓ

Choose the best answer for questions 6–8.

6. The is _____ the 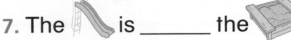. (MG 2.4)

   Ⓐ above   Ⓒ behind

   Ⓑ far from   Ⓓ in front of

7. The is _____ the . (MG 2.4)

   Ⓐ below   Ⓒ next to

   Ⓑ in front of   Ⓓ down from

8. The is _____ the . (MG 2.4)

   Ⓐ above   Ⓑ behind   Ⓒ far from   Ⓓ below

WRITE Math ▶ Explain your answer for questions 9–10.

9. Write how many tiles are needed to finish the pattern.

(0–ᴨ SDAP 2.1)

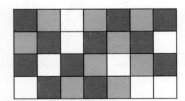

_____  _____

Cross out the paintings that do not match the clues. Circle the answer.

(MG 2.4)

10. Mia paints a square above a circle. She paints a triangle above the square.
Which painting is Mia's?

Chapter 20

from THE WORLD ALMANAC FOR KIDS

Cars

Not all cars have 4 wheels. Here is an example, a cable car! You can still ride one today. Have you ever been on a cable car?

California Problem Solving

ALMANAC Fact

The first cable cars in the United States were on Clay Street in San Francisco.

cable car

FACT·ACTIVITY

❶ Color the cars to show a pattern. Use 2 colors.

❷ Color the wheels to show a pattern. Use 3 colors.

❸ Color the cars to show a pattern. Use 2 colors.
Color the wheels to show a pattern. Use 3 colors.

TALK Math Explain the 2 patterns you made in Exercise 3.

First Cars

The first cars did not look like cars today. What did the first car look like? Look at the picture. What figures do you see?

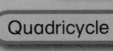

Quadricycle

FACT·ACTIVITY

Use circles, triangles, squares, and rectangles to design your own car.

How many did you draw?

_____ triangles _____ circles _____ squares _____ rectangles

TALK Math Describe your car. Show and explain the different figures you chose.